My Mother,
the Butcher

My Mother, the Butcher

Poems

Gerard Robledo

The TRP Chapbook Series, No. 15

 **trp**

TRP: THE UNIVERSITY PRESS OF SHSU
HUNTSVILLE, TEXAS 77341

Library of Congress Cataloging-in-Publication Data
Names: Robledo, Gerard author
Title: My mother, the butcher : poems / Gerard Robledo.
Description: First edition | Huntsville, Texas : TRP: The University Press
    of SHSU, 2025. | Series: The TRP chapbook series
Identifiers: LCCN 2025006199 (print) | LCCN 2025006200 (ebook) | ISBN
    9781680034226 trade paperback | ISBN 9781680034233 ebook
Subjects: LCGFT: Poetry
Classification: LCC PS3618.O3354 M9 2025 (print) | LCC PS3618.O3354
    (ebook) | DDC 811/.6--dc23/eng/20250305
LC record available at https://lccn.loc.gov/2025006199
LC ebook record available at https://lccn.loc.gov/2025006200

FIRST EDITION

Cover art courtesy of Victoria Cast Iron Cookware © 2024
Author photo by Kat Carey

Cover design by Cody Gates, Happenstance Type-O-Rama
Interior design by Maureen Forys, Happenstance Type-O-Rama

Printed and bound in the United States of America
First Edition Copyright: 2025

TRP: The University Press of SHSU
Huntsville, Texas 77341
texasreviewpress.org

Contents

As children, we believe
our parents are gods.

Murder Ballad

your feet flat keeping time
against my belly pushing me up
until I open like an umbrella

inside our home heels balance
my pelvis the unseen spur
digging where hip meets flexor

a weak point your body found in me
push too hard I fold like a plastic chair
not enough I shatter my face

across your knees my eyes everywhere
yours cataloging my giggles
the smile's equator of teeth

you buckle and I tumble into sixteen
through strewn Bartles & Jaymes
the ashtray our kitchen your song

cuts at my throat for men who won't
love you your children your girth
there you sing with full throat

the forty-year earworm
these bloody lyrics murder slowly
from your lips *You ruined my life*

and all that made happiness
cleaved never to sing
verses of love your child needs

A Sunday Without Eucharist

Truth can never be told so as to be understood, and not be believed.
—WILLIAM BLAKE, Proverbs of Hell

He drew a bead on my falling tears, then raised
his innocent palms—shields of flesh.
Your fingers split our hands,

    like spoons into raw chicken—another nick
    in the bones. With a pinch and twist of your nails
    at our triceps, outside the priest's view,

you jangled two marionettes
behind the last teen to cadenced footfalls
through the church hall. A sacred space

    diffused with dancing shadows, squealing
    guitars, the pop and skip of a worn record
    a projected young toe

over a shotgun trigger—the barrel up
under a boy's chin, then his face blown off.
Some might say "clean off," but it wasn't clean:

    bits of flesh, teeth, skull splattered
    across bathroom ceiling, wall, then mirror.
    Over yellowing crime scene photos,

an echoing voice boomed,
This is where Satan lives,
in your errant music,

    twisting between words. A rare Sunday
    we spent together, squandered
    trying to make us good

Christian men. Rejoice. A Sunday deprived
of Eucharist, no digestible Body-of-Christ,
just teenage lives smeared

    across our faces—this memory,
    now called an incident.
    To say there was only fear

in that sanctuary is to say that water rages
in a river. With that same fury,
my brother tried to dam my eyes. That night

    Satan was not in our music
    nor in that hall, but you were
    there clenching our wrists.

Meditation on a Ritual

A girlfriend once laughed, I packed a fresh lunch
for Helena every day at fourteen years old.
But I only have the one to her three—
one is such a finite number. I didn't tell her
though, there's a strange peaceful comfort
to this ritual: the slow cadence of blade
splitting carrots, its halves open like hands
cupping water; the shearing sound
slicing slivers of cucumber—
scissors through wrapping paper,
the bounce of small green globes
into a container, eventually to burst
with cooling sweet juice in her mouth.
The dwindling moments of my usefulness;
not my need, but ability to still do
something that makes both of us
happy. Li-Young Lee wrote the sound
his mother's comb made against hair,
the long grain and winter vegetables
in the morning, love between parents; I can't
help but meditate on my morning acts
that will eventually be shared
with someone else she loves
early in the morning.

A Miron Zownir Photo (Moscow, 1998)

My monochromatic parents hang
in their wedding photo next to the front door,
above the champagne rosé carpet,

a matted ruddy path to the bathroom, kitchen, fridge.
An anxious fluttering of fluorescent bulbs
dims across their faces—

a capturing in black and white.
But everything is in black and white:
memories, dreams, my selective colorblindness,

the polka-dotted skirt contrasting
the clinal variation of dirt from ankle to pale thigh,
though nothing is as black as the blood behind her shoulder

and trailing head. The concrete steps
wobbling her temple and eyebrow. It's unfortunate,
the cigarette that burned through her knuckle

couldn't wake her before her cart was stolen,
or her children left, but it's only a photo.
Though, maybe it's just about this,

finding signs she's home too, the anxiousness—
a slog through the evidence:
unlocked front door, television blaring,

every light on; the Truman show of my life
on a CCTV in the bathroom.
There's my mother, again. She's waiting

to be put out of her misery, again,
waiting for the ease of the slow blade
behind my palm's pressure. Her groans

greet me with churning alcohol—curdling
formaldehyde in a distended belly, preserving
this blasphemous scene, like a pig's head in fixative.

Her drool mingles with the yellow toilet base.
The scent of vomit, bile:
boiled eggs, bologna, iron—

parenthood beneath my nose
after a night out. She's poured into the hallway,
deserted to crawl. Flinting knees against rug,

leaving prints like a bleeding doe in dirty snow.
To find her, another coming-of-age ritual:
sling my pickled mother off the floor, over

my shoulder, dangling like my first kill, first blood.
The first voice I felt caress my ear and lull me,
now callous, melting on my neck; dribbling with shit

held behind half a century of just-missed successes
and unrequited loves that are my fault. Emptying herself:
words and spit down my spine, pooling.

I drown myself in what remains of her,
the persistent slithering of a running toilet
that whips my earlobe—Saturdays, circa 1998.

A Pillow Made of Knuckles

Holding my breath, I check for warm drool.
Are your eyes still rolling under their lids,

like searchlights draped with thin skins?
My ear pressed over your chest—

a stethoscope. My breath across
your shoulder, lips in your palm.

I feel the long lines of your sputtering air
tunnel your lungs, then a pause: everything tightens

and closes—the trauma of birth, watching
your waterlogged lungs wrung out,

the exodus through your mother—
a reverse drowning.

The last connection
with your mother—the umbilical cord,

oxygen, nutrients. Your breath
must happen, now. Mother's

blood and oxygen no longer available.
Exiting your first suffocation

with a slap, your forced
first breath taken makes me

yearn for thirty more years,
carrying your tiny wails and voice

inside me, behind my breastbone,
pattering next to my heart. That ardor halts

my razor's horizontal movement when I shave.
Now you kick off the blankets I secured

under your delicate elbows, curl yourself
inward—my tangled pill bug,

knees tucked, hands wedged between sheet
and cheek: a pillow made of knuckles.

Their rounding end, almost brash,
jutting with the edge of breath,

like a sudden infant death: the syndrome
I still fear at your twelfth birthday.

Thank God she's not a man
and she's half-White, my mother said.

Uncountable number of breaths taken
since your birth. How many until my last? Following

the dependable raise and drop of your chest,
the quakes in my palms steady. I use

your sweat to anoint myself with a cross—
two lines intersecting above my eyes

where only I feel its presence,
the spot my mother's thumb carved,

while you rest, huddled,
like you've been crying alone all night.

Off-Brand Man

It's what makes a man a man. Veins
should be clear and bold as the printed daily special,

according to my mother, glaring at my arms
in high school—her voice oscillating between disgust

and disappointment with my paunchy extremities.
The veins lost in the 70/30 meat mix that I am—

discounted for quick sale, never on the top shelf,
maybe in an easily passed bin, or at least in a plastic bag.

This off brand version of man—an acquired taste
for women who've loved me, like gnawing on gristle and fat.

No, a real man's hands and forearms
are a fleshy facsimile of the god of thunder's:

swing the hammer, spark skin with touch,
and pull closer my woman's hips.

A topographical abundance of veins
raises the skin, drives muscle

against tendon and bone—the center, creamy, fatty
marrow, savory flavor coating the mouth, a velvet thickness

mashed between cheek and gum. The tongue's tip
throbs with the same pulse beating through

intricate weavings from fingertip to elbow,
a cuffed sleeve meets bicep—the romantic tourniquet

maintaining pumped girth where it matters.
The DNA of anguish is watching

my body spill over its edges. *No woman*
resists a man who cooks for them,

my brother said. *It's your only hope to find love*
without a man's body.

Skin

Behind my back, you
    ask me to give my hand—
its forceful discipline withheld,

    only the tenderness of touch released. *My skin,*
    you say,
        is like Mommy's, not yours.
Your skin is dark, not mine.
        Mine, like her

    last name: rough, awkward,
and ends with a hard consonant
    when you constantly say *it's dark.* I shove
    my arm further back, palm exposed,
closer to you,
        Mija, miralo bien.
        Somos iguales,
        only lighter shades.
    Fine, but your eyes
    turn and follow the American
sprawl streaming passed us.

    I think back to your mother and I
    in bed: lights out,
a black room except her

    mirroring the moon's sparkle.

My muted hue,
    a worn wooden floor,
        spine creaking under her steps.

        Your skin, the tan milk that never sours
nor sparkles in the moonlight.

The Last Days of Summer

During summer, mornings are cold.
　My body cracks—
a bundle of weak twigs across a boy's knee.

Surprisingly, I'm forty-ish and not diabetic.
Still, when I stretch for my sandals and shirt,
　the worn cartilage and bone rubbing

together clear any doubts—splintering the daybreak
　like a rooster's call, a cock shouting behind my grandmother
at 5 a.m. *Dios*, she'd say, waking early just to watch

　the day careen past. My child needs
to rouse herself slowly
　with the kindred voices of other children

and adults with their hands up
　the asses of sock puppets
on PBS kids—that bent-over Kermit

　meme burned into my mind: his hand
hole rosebudding like pimento
　out of an olive, eliciting a desire

for a morning cigarette. But it's only Tuesday;
　there are still flat pancakes and fake bacon
to throw in the microwave while I lumber

in the kitchen, preparing her lunch, missing my curlers
and vinyl slippers. My music just out of earshot:
   sometimes it's the ten years I lost, Passion Pit and Justice

sparking the electronic mornings; other times,
   it's the teen years I wish I were more
confident in, stuck in a loop—Ian Curtis and Iggy Pop

   stepping out and spotting trains, with the living dead,
pale faced, black lips, and fishnets staggering into a Denny's
at 3 a.m. I *Choose Life.* Now, at forty, I need her

structure and sobriety to keep me accountable—I'm not.
   Sometimes she'll creep from behind: me, crisscross
applesauce at the coffee table. Her arms overtake

   as best a child can. Tiny fingers work around my throat
the other hand thrust in my armpit. I'm vulnerable
   to her tickles and questions. *Will you ever stop working?*

Failure to answer distresses her. My grandmother
   climbs out of her mouth, kitchen knife in hand,
following that question. She wants me to be everything:

   a good father and mother, nurturing like taught,
and masculine like I never saw; sew her skirt
   and knees together, then ignore the tampon

I'll eventually slide under the door.
   For her, I'll pretend I'm a dumb rock of a man
while I caress bruises and bake dinner.

It's what my grandmother taught me while decrying
my mother's incapability. It's what I'll show my brothers
men do with an iron and starch. Still, no answer.

When will I stop? My half-White daughter
with strands of red, brown, and gold hair mixing
in the early blue-morning-half-light. I can't help

but think of Molly Ringwald in *Pretty in Pink*
reprimanding her father for his lethargic mornings
when she serves me a brunch of biscuits drizzled

with honey and a cocktail: her last Dreamsicle
and Topo Chico over ice.
But she doesn't know her mom left us—

me. I miss her when gone, now
near twelve, do I realize this. The parenting part
of being a parent: schedules, recipes,

and implied domestication raises my profile
for women I don't know, but it won't
balance the guilt of freedom, my exploits:

Eat, Drink, & Fuck
stenciled in lavender on whitewashed shiplap,
not found at Pier 1, but maybe Family Dollar.

Text Message to an Ex-girlfriend: Mother's Day

Today is not a good day for people
like us. The yellowing photos
shared on the internet, the many posts,
profound statements of admiration, wanted recipes

handed down over generations. Distressing
for some single moms like you. A third week
in a row, no break. Maybe a day
without the kids is a better gift

than trying to entertain them? For forty years,
I've lied about this day to everyone,
a false representation of a filled life—
a taxidermied child. Now

I can't see anything but the painful truth—
my mother's bloody apron,
the butcher. She wears sections of my childhood
like outlined choice cuts

across her breasts: loin, ribs, brain;
the tender bits, ego, heart, emotion,
things that slide and stain
red with slow movement

on wood, then easily wrapped
in newsprint, sold at cost. I lay my carcass
across this bed, collecting on the clogged drain—
my fat blocking the escape of blood and salty water.

Coritos de Machismo

my arms a warm bath around her
slight frame pulling us together slender fingers

file between ribs a point through my heart and lungs
releasing my breath exorcizing me my pulse

a metronome resonating with baritone lullaby
above her temple our days end

grabbing serenity with a cheek easing
into my chest a pond of drool

collecting the weeping moon her hand
cupping my breath thumb skimming mustache

::

wake to pins and needles
through my hand her body
compressing nerves
a throbbing cognizance
I'll dream often alone
when she is gone grown
holding her own no longer

in need of my droning heartbeat
my pulse greets my grandmother
blanketed in sod   my voice
a memory reverberating

my child synchronizing with her
emerging when her days are slow

::

mirror my grandmother's broken hands
dust the hair from my child's face
caress forehead every night

a small pillow my name embroidered in red
next to her head we sang coritos
the words dribbled from my lips

little gifts to God gathering
with the streetlight in her bed every bit of me
piecemealed by her buckling fingers

grazing breath at my ears
the only cashmere ever known
love a child before she's born

The Last Days of Summer for an Alcoholic

Been working hard and searching for God,
but ended up at the strip club instead

are the words of a woman I follow
on social media. I don't know her

or the intricacies of being that remove her clothing,
but those words are doppelgängers of my own—

a specter of my existence. But I'm lying
when I don't admit I fear her

life: a job with no pay or medical
and a cancerous child. Still,

my God's a mirage,
a hallucination only

seen with dying thirst—
the spirit dragged from red waters,

an overturned dredged bottle. Fear
doesn't break my pour before my daughter

sleeps. This time is a soft, red comfort
filling my glass. Under my feet,

fragmenting eggs: shell forced through the albumen,
penetrating the vitelline membrane,

cleaving the sunshine with tiny shards
of calcium carbonate—

the composition of bone
also lacerates. Her beady little eyes

shift past the glass to mine, she drops respect
in the garbage. Dialing my childhood,

my mother—the condemnation of god, the ace
in her packet. My delayed yellowing eyes

refusing to slow me, but her ten-year-old feet
stop at the threshold, turning from my slurring.

No God to fence her with dread
or halt my decanting. The alcohol

seeps from my wrists
so I nurse myself—the slurp,

suckle on lip of glass
in search of an ease

to parenthood; the easiest answer
that keeps my clothes on

and my daughter from knowing
how a dollar is a stand-in for love,

self-respect, and success—an answer
to faith and the American dream.

What's Left

Before the sink fills
      With filthy
Grey bubbles
      I lay the bleeding
Tomato on my toast
      Wipe her
Plate clean
      Into the trash and palm

The sandwich crust
      Its brown
Edges sprout
      A seam of Day-Glo

Cheese and false meat
      They mash

Between the soggy napkin
      And dry skin

Sweeping the ends
      Into my mouth
With thumb

      Something for myself
From what's left

      Reminiscent of my mother

Over the stove

Scraping together
The remains
Broken tortillas

Bits of cabbage and
crumbles of meat

In the recessed center

Of a saucer

The smallest plate

A debris filled crater

Her sons'
Engorged bellies
Slowly rising and falling

With heavy breath
Splayed across

The carpet absorbing

The television's radiation

In the distance
My daughter's

Words shear my ears

You're just like Grandma

Always eating the scraps

The Ephemeral Lighthouse

Just outside my fingernails, the lights,
distant passing cars on the highway—a chain

of small lighthouses, a measure of proximity
to safety, turning and fleeting from my balcony.

Alone this Saturday night. Through the sprouting
leaves of Spring, their gleam suspends

the cruelest times. Again, my daughter's gone.
Seven years and running on the weekend rotation.

Inside our apartment, it's already "Texas warm."
There's the moldy, smoky smell of a motel,

of the leather binding of a Gideon Bible,
and not my home. Just over my pulse,

the hocking circulation of blood
in my ear, the wooden floor

creaking under my heels.
The tinny music cracking my phone

with the voice of a forty-year-dead singer—
something about love tearing us apart

and different roads into the night.
Can you hear the disconnection,

the click and slink of two metal pieces
unclasping, separating the safety belt

to make space for herself? She fills a wine glass
with strawberry lemonade and sparkling water.

The pink liquid swirls, its pulp settles
to the floor of her drink. Her pour echoes mine

without the alcohol or shakes. From the distance
to her bedroom, I hear the approaching clip-clopping

of heels and incoherent teen chatter. Is it unsettling,
or do I not want my construction-paper likeness

to fall apart under the scrutiny of its words,
Best. Daddy. Ever? Did you know

pouring alcohol over colored paper will bleed the ink
and make beautiful works of alcoholic art

but will destroy the paper in the process?
Paper now as fragile as gold leaf,

this process as precious as making a child
in another country. It's still nothing

when I remember I'm not an immigrant
mother. Though sometimes I am

just as lost in expectations
along a path I must translate into

a language that escapes—my mother
never carved me a Rosetta Stone,

only doused me in cheap beer and left
me a car wreck considered from afar.

The Summer of Children

She sleeps while I write this, four whiskeys deep.
After five years, the routine of her leaving me
for three days, returning happy on Monday is not normal,

though I tell everyone it is. It makes me a "good dad."
The silence is still unnerving. By the third day,
I enter her room, absorb the sounds muted when she is present—

the negative to our life. My breathing, an unsettling
crescendo and decrescendo—a ten-year refrain.
Holding the plush toys that comfort her at night, I try

to soothe myself with the glowing star
on her bedroom ceiling. I feel the neighbor's fighting
through the walls: his knuckles raking ear to chin—caking rouge;

the drunks blathering about God, time, and the clerk
ejecting them through the door. An anxious pulse in my chest,
yearning to be vacuous. Sitting there, aware, time is encroaching—

this space soon to be a transparent exposure.
The third weekend of the month, two days away—I hang
a vacancy sign in her window

only I can see, like the flickering neon
of the seedy motel my mother and I stayed in
with one eye open, hiding from her merciless husband.

She met him four Coors deep, then married
after five weeks. The Jesus tattooed on his forearm
oversaw the halfway house he lived in. He pissed, sweat,

and bled the Bible, methadone, and communal love.
She drank with the dropping sun; then he beckoned her
to bed. No time for a routine to build a home

before heaving her down the hall, face shaking
next to seven-year-old feet. No happy Mondays,
no good nights keeping me from tracing her outlined path

onto my own. The last days of summer, the end to all
that was good—a smile from May to September. I fear
my child will not return home like me. Though

I want and dread this—outgrow me, my missteps,
and acknowledge I was always there,
though, with whiskey in hand.

How to Raise a Poet

Take him on a first date, set a standard.

Don't save money for babysitters.

Don't save money.

Let his brown brothers tell him he's adopted.

Laugh with them while he cries.

When his knee is split open like a summer watermelon, make sure to finish applying your makeup before taking him to the emergency room.

On the way to the emergency room, take an extra trip to your boyfriend's to explain why you can't go out, so he can see you're bleeding son—proof you're not cheating on him.

Tell him your truth: *Everyone was grown and growing. I thought you didn't need me anymore.* He was five.

Let your parents raise him.

Never finish paying for promises made.

Allow braces to be repossessed like your Porsche.

Be wasted when he comes home in the evenings. His age doesn't matter because it's consistency that counts.

Show that love and relationships can be impulsive and never fully found.

Let everyone else be the parent.

Television raises him better than you anyway.

Let his bipolar brother give him counsel.

Leave on vacation without telling anyone.

After four days, call and tell him and his brothers you're on a cruise and won't be back for two more weeks.

Forget to buy groceries before you leave on that cruise.

Marry a drug addict.

Marry men you barely know.

Walk away when he needs you most. Make sure you do it several
   times in his life. Again, consistency is key.

Pretend he doesn't cry himself to sleep alone.

Question his sexuality behind his back.

Force religion on him, then question his education.

Never read to him.

Tell him he's just like his father after saying his father was unfaithful.

Ask him for money when he gets his first job because he owes you.

Ask him for money when he's a single parent scraping to make ends meet.

Force his tongue to contort to an accent he fears, then judge him for it.

Call him a sellout.

Tell him he's too White now.

When his finger gets crushed in the door at a lawyer's office, forget to ask questions about what happened and how to sue them.

Tell him he's getting fat.

Tell him he's getting too dark in the summer.

Speak of the evils of women.

Drink excessively.

Compare him to others.

Let his sexist, racist brother mentor him because he's the eldest.

Rarely say I love you and remind him he was born a sinner.

Make sure the word proud is not part of your lexicon.

Allow the water and electricity bill to not be paid.

Did I say spend the money on booze?

Eat from a church food box regularly.

Become a hoarder: two years of mail piled into stacks on the dining table because they're important enough to keep but not resolve.

Remind him that a shower is a luxury when the water gets shut off again.

Teach him payday loans are normal as long as nothing new happens.

Things always happen.

Set the bar really low.

Your friends and their kids will always come first.

Drink inside while he swims with people he doesn't know, people you barely know.

Leave him with the judgmental aunt who has disdain for him while you go on dates regularly.

By a Porsche, then fail to pay for the good school you put him into.

Tell him he didn't need that school. Do that to him twice.

Never forget that you come first.

Let him find you on the bathroom floor, vomit on your breath, piss in your jeans, his heart spread everywhere around you.

And who cares if he walks in on you making out with yet another man, hand between your legs and up your skirt?

Choose your boyfriends over him.

When one of your boyfriends beats the hell out of him in the front yard, make sure to remind him that it was his fault.

Believe your boyfriends over your child.

Impose everything you can on him. Make it a constant flow like rain into the gutter.

After all of this, expect your child to care for you when you're dying and on hospice.

Be upset and blame him when he says, *I won't do this anymore.*

Mother's Day

There's nothing left here
to say really means it's your turn

to speak because I hope to hell
you've been listening and not just waiting

to talk through me, against the alarm
that gives way to a reminder—my daughter,

another track meet in the early a.m.,
when you are still sleeping,

her mother's back to her husband
in their dead bed before their day breaks.

You slowly push off the past
with an unease, an upward launch

from the bottom of a murky lake,
through the water and the warm currents

against you and your comfortable responses:
I tried my best, I was doing what I knew how

to do with what I had been given,
but never *I'm sorry.* And *I'm sorry* is still

not there to hold me up or bury
my foot into, but your question,

What should I have done? pushes the metal
corner of my spatula against the smoking

cast iron and tofu—my stand-in for meat,
something to sink my teeth into

without the iron-heavy taste;
a desire for what my body needs.

Before my shoulders give, you exit
water, admitting, *I should have just been there.*

Acknowledgments

Many thanks to the editors and readers of the following journals, in which these poems first appeared, in slightly different versions.

Oyster River Pages: "A Pillow Made of Knuckles"

The Thing Itself: "Skin"

Vox Populi Sphere: "Off-Brand Man"

My gratitude to J. Bruce Fuller, Charlie Tobin, and TRP for making this debut chapbook a reality and for their patience with all my delays.

Thank you to those mentors who encouraged me to keep writing at every moment I needed: Philip Arevalo, Jane Foche-Hansen, Kathleen Peirce, Cyrus Cassells, Reggie Scott Young, and Eduardo C. Corral. There are two people to whom I owe so much and who are no longer with us: my poetry mother, Carol Coffee Reposa, who pushed me to get my MFA, opened so many doors, and kept Helena and me fed and hopeful when times were the hardest; and Mike Burton, the professor father I needed, our conversations and your support I valued so much.

Endless gratitude to my dearest friends who kept me excited about my writing, shared thoughts, and most importantly, said they are proud of me: Michael Cepek, Jerid Morris, Ron Pollard, Laurie Ann Gurrero, Micha Larson, J. Bruce Fuller, Miranda Ramirez, Lauren Lark, Matthew Tavares, Lila Espinoza, Andrew McFadyen-Ketchum, Stephen Andrus, Lee Williams, Richard Boada, and last but never least Joshua Robbins.

Thank you, Allegra Castro, for everything. No list is long enough.

To Helena, thank you for being the bright, wonderful, and compassionate daughter you are. There's nothing worth it without you.

About the Author

GERARD ROBLEDO is a Mexican American poet from San Antonio and an Immigrant son. He holds an MFA in Creative Writing from the University of Texas at El Paso and is Assistant Professor of English at Palo Alto College. His Spanish language poetry translations, poetry, and book reviews have appeared in *Voices de la Luna*, *The Texas Observer*, *Oyster River Pages*, *Solstice Magazine*, *Poetrybay*, *Vox Populi*, and others. He is a Macondo Writers' Workshop Fellow, and a recipient of the 2020 Eduardo Corral Emerging Latinx Writers Mentorship.

The TRP Chapbook Series

Series Editor: J. Bruce Fuller

The TRP Chapbook Series highlights work by emerging authors who have not yet released their first full-length book in addition to established authors working on shorter projects.

BOOKS IN THIS SERIES:

Praise for *My Mother, the Butcher*

"Penned with intense and captivating energy, Gerard Robledo's *My Mother, the Butcher* is deeply pleasurable to read, even as it evokes painful family dynamics. In these poems, mundane moments are rendered in a way that reveals the intensity of feeling and dire stakes beneath them. I feel in this book the aches and pressures of parenthood, the living ongoingness of childhood wounds, and the gift and burden of poetry as a way to make a song of so much grief. Here the self is a threshold across which inheritances barrel concurrently, in and out, forward and back. A gorgeous collection—visceral, musical, propulsive, and vivid in ways that wow me again and again."

—**GABRIELLE BATES**, author of *Judas Goat*

"Gerard Robledo's vulnerability and self-awareness are striking and brutal— *'You ruined my life/* and all that made happiness/cleaved never to sing/verses of love your child needs.' *My Mother, the Butcher* is a decisive portrayal of a family, and Robledo is a skilled observer, 'sling my pickled mother off the floor & over/my shoulder, dangling like my first kill, first blood./The first voice I felt caress my ear & lull me,/now callous, melting on my neck.' In the face of trauma and nostalgia, Robledo finds redemption in the mundane forging a hopeful path forward."

—**RUBEN QUESADA**, author of *Brutal Companion*

"Filled with tenderness and lyrical beauty, *My Mother, The Butcher*, paints a searing portrait of childhood abuse and its aftermath, interrogating the way trauma is inherited, internalized, and extended across generations. In poems that are carved out of lived experience, Robledo constructs a complex masculinity, examining fatherhood, Mexican-American heritage, and the damage incurred in pursuit of the American dream. A deeply felt, ruthlessly honest quest for healing and forgiveness."

—**KAI CARLSON-WEE**, author of *Rail*

"*My Mother, the Butcher* invites you in for a home-cooked meal, just don't expect your typical choice cut meat, though there's plenty of beef. There's tofu, veggies, and 'fake meat' prepared by a poet who, as a single dad, must 'be everything: a good father & mother' to his daughter against the forces of his own dysfunctional family. Machismo, nourishing mothers, identity politics are on the cutting board and nothing is spared evisceration. Robledo's debut collection cuts through the fat, muscle, gristle and marrow 'in search of an ease / to parenthood.'"

—**JOHN OLIVARES ESPINOZA**, author of *The Date Fruit Elegies*

"Gerard Robledo's debut collection, *My Mother, the Butcher*, begins with a 'Murder Ballad' and the story of 'how much it costs to love a child.' The cost of love in these poems, however, is not a nurturing one: it's a reckoning, 'my mother's bloody apron, the butcher. She wears sections of my body & childhood, outlines choice cuts . . . ' an understanding of how speakers caught in cycles of traumas try not to repeat the violence of the past, but rather embrace a tenderness against the butchering."

—**RICHARD BOADA**, author of *We Find Each Other in the Darkness*